# ABOUT THE AUTHOR

Fritzinie Lavoile is a twenty-year-old Haitian poet whose literary prowess extends beyond her years. Her poetry is a celebration of her roots and a tribute to her homeland, Haiti, first generation immigrants, as well as a confirmation of faith in God and love for family.

Through *Haitian Views Through the Glass House*, she extends a heartfelt invitation to immigrants or anyone in search of inspiration, to find solace within these lines.

Her debut poetry collection, *Ruminative Words*, was released in 2022 and is available for purchase on Amazon.

# Haitian Views Through the Glass House

Fritzinie Lavoile

Lavoile Literature Loft LLC

Haitian Views Through the Glass House

Paperback ISBN: 979-8-9875475-3-3
Hardcover ISBN: 979-8-9875475-4-0
E-Book ISBN: 979-8-9875475-5-7

Cover design by Janni Pillerva

Published by Lavoile Literature Loft LLC

www.FritzinieLavoile.com

For permission requests, please contact:

Fritzinie Lavoile
Fritzinielavoile@gmail.com

Trigger warning:

This collection delves into serious themes including racism, violence, death, loss, family strife, and depression, offering critical social commentary. Reader discretion is advised as these topics may not be suitable for all audiences.

# CONTENTS

Provenance     1

In the Wake of Calamity     36

Mirrored Whispers     61

Subtle Blessings     80

Glimpses of Home     102

# Provenance

I don't know the Haiti that you've all heard about.
So, allow me to introduce you to
the Haiti beyond the headlines and social media feeds.
The Haiti that's not trailing behind every charity event.

I don't think you've heard about my Haiti.
The Haiti where your neighbors
can lend you a dollar or a tablespoon of butter.
You don't know the type of generosity and understanding
that rests on everyone's shoulder.
It's a land filled with entrepreneurs, creatives,
carving paths to support their families.
A community of farmers, street vendors
fighting for their children's future.

Haiti is beautiful music that dances through your soul.
It's a flavorful food that always leaves you craving more.
It's where strangers form bonds closer than family.
A little island that enriches
more than a glass house of fortune.

Did you hear about my Haiti?
Where the oceans gleam in the deepest hues of blues.
Its majestic mountains reach out to the skies
kissing the floating clouds.
The flawless beaches mimic see-through glass.
Where there's never a starless night sky.

A land where goats roam freely, dogs run wild,
and a chicken and toddler are best friends.

Yes, the history is sad.
Yet, the people are brave.
They continue to fight despite
being neglected and rejected.
Despite being starved
of the peace they deserve.

I don't know the Haiti they've told you about.
For in the words of our beloved Mika Ben, it's laid,

*"Ayiti se yon manman*
*ki konn sa yo rele doulè*
*On fanm ki djanm*
*on fanm vanyan*
*menm si li konnen*
*li pa pafè."*

Haiti is a beautiful woman
who's been through a whole lot.
Who always makes sure her children
walk with their heads up proud.

\*\*\*

I was raised with
flavors that told
tales of my childhood.

Dlo sikré, pen a manba.
Dipping my bread in the kafé a lèt,
a ritual which few know of.
Every night wondering if I was going to be
Mixing pen avec avwann or labouyi bannann.

Du riz- so versatile
it can be paired with almost anything.
Pwa nwa, pwa wouj, pwa blan.
Legume- a medley of lively hues,
Nourishing our bodies, chasing away the blues.

Fritay- a carnival of flavors.
Griyo, akra, bannann pézé, marinad.
With pikliz always in hand.

Bouyon- a treat no matter the season.
Vyann and viv simmering slow.
Fèy, yanm, bannann, bóy, trip kabrit, pye kabrit,
epis and a touch of finesse.

Soup Joumou- a New Year's gift.
Symbolizing resilience, independence.
Kawót, pómdétè, chou, each spoonful resonates.
Reminding me of Haitian history and strength.

\*\*\*

If I were to return to my childhood home. I would hope to walk through that big blue gate, entering that front yard where my father sat bracing himself for the second wave of Mother Nature's wrath. I would hope to see the outdoor chairs, where I sat under those starry night skies alongside my neighbor. Where our voices mingled with the breeze as we shared our youthful worries.

I would hope to walk through that black metal door. Into the cement walls that supported and raised me… listening intently…hoping to catch the echoes of my laughter. Tracing the stains that my tears and my blood left.

Two bedrooms that lay across each other. One bathroom sitting right at the center. A kitchen, where I would soak my clothes as my small body leaned over the sink, tiptoed on a stool, washing the dishes. The stove that heated cold water for my morning showers. The dining room table that witnessed my tireless efforts, all night snot nosed determined to memorize my homework.

Sunlight seeped through every hole by day. While gas lanterns and candles illuminated from within by night. I would hope the concrete walls still sprouted white mold like it was spreading magical dust.

Oh, how I wish I had scraped some off when I had the chance, to carry the essence of my home, spreading it through this lifeless air.

\*\*\*

The first time I saw a corpse, wasn't within the hospital walls. The first time I saw a corpse, wasn't amidst a somber funeral procession. The first time I saw a corpse was on the street, as I walked hand-in-hand with my mother on my way to elementary school.

There he lay, in a pool of his dried blood. The people walked around him, barely casting a glance. Only the flies seemed to care. Daring to fly close to his nose checking for signs of life. Or perhaps, they were indulging in his decaying scent-it's not like I could tell the difference.

My mind ponders the state of my country. Imagining her also an abandoned corpse present on the street. Imagining her spirit praying for a touch of compassion. Imagining her patiently awaiting the collective hands that would come together, offering them both a rightful place of solace.

***

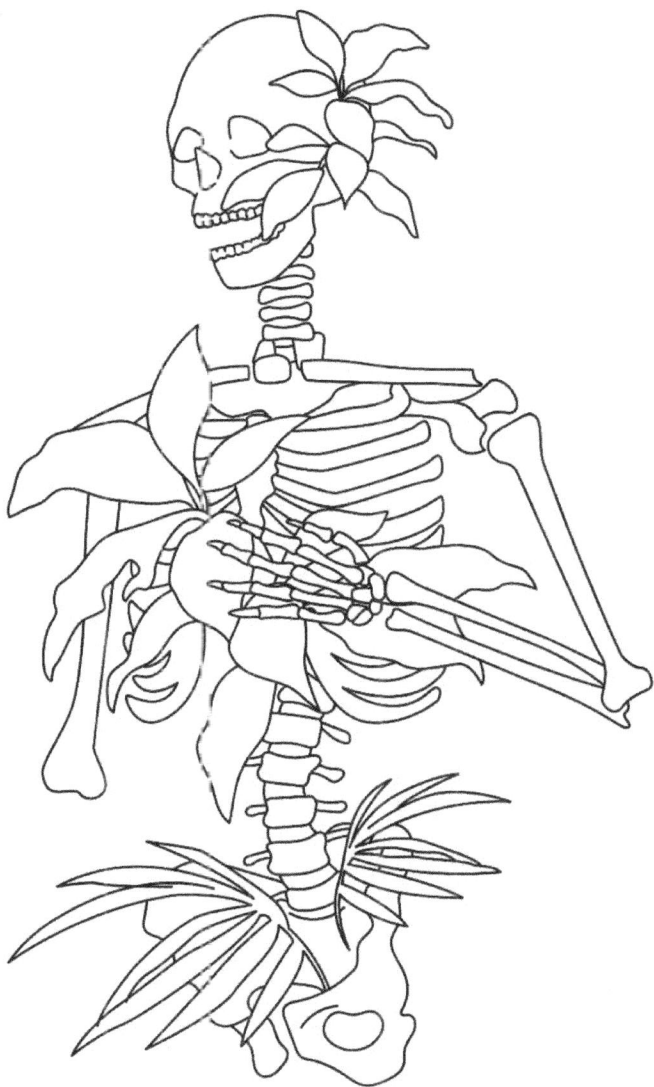

It's been six long years since I set foot in Haiti. It was four before that. Each passing year, I hope and pray: *Is this the time when I finally get to touchdown and kiss the land that made me?*

Then my mom tells me how things have worsened since my absence. I wonder: *When will the peace that I grew up with come back?*

Perhaps I was the final straw. Maybe it watched as I packed my bags and never returned and thought that I abandoned it. Maybe it missed me so much it decided to run after me and lost its way back home.

*For my land has not been the same since I departed.*

\*\*\*

*My homeland teeters*
*on the brink of fading*
*into a mere fairytale.*
*Gradually slipping*
*into the abyss*
*of distant memories.*

\*\*\*

My father reminisces about the good old days.
When he would hitchhike to school.
When the nation believed in its youth.
When the nation invested in its youth.

He speaks now of a nation lost.
Where the youth no longer nurture the land.
Where the youth yearn for weapons in their hands.

My father reminisces about his childhood.
His eyes ignite with a glimmer,
firing remnants of bittersweet pain.
A longing for a Haiti that is forever changed.

He titles himself fortunate
to have known his nation back then.
He feels sorrow for our people
who will never witness that Haiti again.

\*\*\*

In a Haiti where its own government fails to nurture progress. Where neighbors turn hostile towards those aspiring for betterment. How can such a land move forward?

The words of unity engraved on our flag often remain a hollow expression, not the guiding principles which we live by.

Our resources, education, land, gold…are ruthlessly stripped away leaving us with the mere title of freedom. But we are far from being free. We are bound by the shackles of self-hatred and self-sabotage.

\*\*\*

When more than twelve years are spent paying for your children's education. When all the rest goes into ensuring a roof over their heads and food on their plates. When you live in a country that scarcely pays its workers.

Can you be faulted for not having the backing to fund college? For not possessing the resources to sell the future to your children?

***

A myriad of brilliant minds stride across that graduation stage into the real world.

They step into the disheartening reality of an empty canvas of opportunities.

Left to wander the streets of Haiti. Left seeking solid ground to land their footing.

So many vibrant souls yearn to illuminate the world.

Yet, where are they to stand? There exists no platform. The spotlight is an abyss. The audience remain hushed and cold, unwilling to lend their voices in encouragement.

\*\*\*

It's not fair to be denied the freedom to speak your native tongue in your school. For them to colonize you and call your culture below proper. Below the standard of class.

I wasn't allowed to speak creole in my school. Speaking improper French deemed you uneducated, unworthy of praise. As if mastering my ancestral language through all the contempt was not a skill deserving of celebration. As if preserving my ancestral dialect amidst all the subjugation was not an act of bravery.

My creole is not a mere derivative of French. It stands on its own. A language that echoes generations of history.
My creole is a symbol of resilience, defiance, and identity.

***

No matter how deeply you love something, you cannot compel it to love itself. While your love and care can foster a nurturing environment, the essence of self-love must spring from within. An inner journey of personal growth and acceptance.

\*\*\*

The language I spoke my first words in
remains embedded in my brain.
It is the one I pray in.
It is the one I love in.

My father holds on to it for dear life
for it carries with it the memories of his home.
My grandmother's tongue is heavy with confidence
even if she can't pour all the English out to fill a sentence.

They take moments to pause
and broken English spills out.
They are creating art
out of unfamiliar sounds.

When the world tries to fill your mouth
with insults towards them,
shoving all the ethnicity and heritage
into the phrase:
*"Go back to where you came from."*

Proudly proclaim:
This accent represents a lineage of power.
It is the force behind a lineage of artists
that crafted the art of tongues.
This accent is proof of the magic we possess.
Proof of the enchantment that we carry.
Proof that we hold the weight of two countries
under the roofs of our mouths.

\*\*\*

I was looking for some
semblance of home in my school,
but it was far from it.
From the cold air that surrounded me
to the fairness of its people.
It stood far apart from the land that I knew.

The teachers held no belt or ruler to hit you.
They didn't check your hair for a bow.
Uniform for wrinkles.
Handwriting for neatness.
Nails for length and dirt.
They even straightened
the curves of my cursive letters
that I spent years perfecting.
Now rearranged and spaces inserted.

\*\*\*

Our silent heroes wear cheeks wet with tears.
Scarred from years of being the shield
Protecting their most precious treasures.
Protecting their sons and daughters who dare to dream.

Running from the country that gave her the soil
to raise her beautiful boy
Running to the country that will give her a chance
to save her little girl.

You might see her marching alone looking like no other.
But she is the mother of many nations.
Deep down wars rage within her.
Each side unshakable feelings
of pride and defeat
certainty and worry
sorrow and joy.

*But through it all she hopes*
*that this new land will provide.*

\*\*\*

Embarking on a journey to distant shores,
leaving behind everything named familiar.
Even if your homeland
brought you immense suffering,
is still a daunting endeavor.

To know that you must start from scratch.
To know that your years of education
will be reduced to insignificance.
Still, embracing your sole opportunity
for a brighter future.

*With conviction that he was destined*
*for something greater…*
*He held a tiny hand*
*determined to create a better life for her.*

\*\*\*

For us, first-generation immigrants,
the journey is far from easy.
We're still learning the lay of the land.
Still tripping over our feet.
Still trying to find the balance
for multiple cultures
for multiple expectations.

No education, no money, no support, no examples.
We must become our own guides and mentors.
From the depths of nothingness,
we must build everything.

In leaving our homelands
we shed the burden of survival.
But in its absence,
we carry the weight of being pioneers.
Shouldering the hopes and dreams
of those who will follow.

\***

It was my aunt who first blazed the trail
opening the path for my grandma.
She, in turn, cleared the way for the rest of us,
and now it's my duty to make room for my mom.

Hand in hand, we ascend together.
All it takes is a small flap of wings.
A flutter of hope and a seat on the plane.

From there, we'll seize the opportunities.
Ignite a storm of progress.
Carry our lineage to greatness.

One generation at a time,
our struggles begin to diminish.
Survival is no longer our sole focus,
but a gateway to a life of abundance.
Our challenges transform into pursuits of luxury,
reflecting the way life should be.

\*\*\*

Immersed in a foreign culture,
where everything around us doesn't relate to us.
Where they hand pick which versions of blackness are
deemed acceptable and worthy of representation.

Where everyday essentials,
from hair products to beauty products,
fail to accommodate our unique complexions.
Where our needs are disregarded,
even when we raise our voices.

Submerged in a new world where no life vests
were stored for the people who mashed
sweat and tears to hold together the vessel
that ripped them out of their mother's womb.

\*\*\*

How can I find a sense of belonging in the classroom,
when faces like mine are scarce to see?

\*\*\*

Surrounded by a world that incessantly reminds me
of my differences, making me feel unwelcome, undesired.

Why must I strive to fit into a world
that callously rejects and excludes me?

I reject the notion of fighting for validation.
Of having to prove my worth and claim my space.

My color, my hair, my gender, my heritage.
Every facet of my being deserves celebration.

\*\*\*

Fritzinie Lavoile

Under the weight of societal pressures,
we are coerced to mute the vibrant hues of our flags.
Modify our hair texture and tone down our voices,
simply to prove that we too deserve fundamental respect.

With each word we acquire from foreign tongues,
we find ourselves drifting
farther away from our true home.

Fear lingers beneath the sun's warm embrace,
for our camouflage may eventually fade,
unveiling the richness of our melanin shade.

***

They wish me to confuse this place with home.
Stripping my culture, leaving strands to roam.
From untangling my curls to smoothing its texture.

My insecurities grew, my self-image misplaced.
Ironed strands that stood straight, as if defying the change.
Resisting the sway, pushing against the tide.

A battle so real, almost tangible.
It lingers around, like a hand that could grasp.
Around me... it hovers.
Tightening its grip around my neck.

Could it ensnare me?
Choke life's breath away?
Depriving my air.
Could it seize me?
Choke my breath away?

> *Black girls, your hair's a crown, each coil a jewel.*
> *Embrace those textures, every kink and curl.*
> *For they tell the stories of your*
> *journey's swirls and tangles.*

\*\*\*

To be a woman, a Black woman,
To be an immigrant, too, what more could be said.
A tapestry of challenges that weren't planned.
Yet, we stand for those just like us.

Filling positions, breaking barriers.
Reclaiming space, creating legacies that surpass.
Showing each other that we too can thrive.

We're not defined by limits, but by the heights we reach.
Our identity transcends, not confined by the norm.
Normalizing black women empowerment
For me, for you, for every Black girl.

\*\*\*

I remember when my background was just that:
something that I would keep in the background.
Rushing to suppress the foreign that flew off my tongue.
So, they would not recognize that I was not of this land.
Praying my darkness away so I could feel attractive.

It's something that this country does to you.
It strips your confidence.
It makes you doubt your intellect,
your beauty, your capability, your strength.

But your intelligence, your essence, your brilliance
Are deeply rooted in you.
And no one and nothing
can take them away from you.

***

Everyone is
Rushing to claim
the dirt that molded me.

Grasping a handful
shoving it in their core
swearing that it was always there.

But the dirt that shaped me runs deep.
Inextricably embedded in my bones, mine to keep.

\*\*\*

I remember the fear that once held me tight.
Hesitant to claim where I came from.
Ashamed to speak of my ancestral land.
Afraid of the looks, laughs and giggles
that I knew would surely follow.

But now look at them,
more than ready to claim my traditions.
As they are shaking their bodies
in hopes that it will move like mine.
Their mouths salivate for the richness of our culture.

Plumping their lips and hips.
Reshaping their sides and thighs.
Wearing our fabrics
they can never match our style.

Before they label my people poor,
I wonder, if they returned all that was unjustly taken
would it even be possible to compare true wealth?
Would they even possess enough to repay their debts?

\*\*\*

Such is the reality here:
they belittle you
strip you of your culture
until shame seeps in.

They teach you to bash and minimize
the people who share your background,
until you yourself aren't brave enough to praise it.

Then, they appropriate,
claiming your traditions and customs as their own.

*They take what they've scorned, and deem it "trendy,"*
*while we're left grappling, lost and empty.*

\*\*\*

Having family in a third world country
is incessant prayer to God every night.
Praying that he will keep them safe.
Praying the kidnappers may show mercy.
That the killers have already satisfied their fill.

It is turning on the news
and feeling the blows of countless disasters.
It is choosing peace of mind
by not picking up the phone.
It is constant worrying.

It is feeling like
you're the sole survivor who escaped tragedy.
It is carrying a burdened conscience,
urging you to go back for your people.
Even as your own wounds remain raw and open.
Even as uncertainty looms over your own life.

***

Pride unfurls in our eyes
when we hear Haiti's name in a movie.
When we hear creole fly off the foreigners' lips
like a child trying to impress their parents
by doing backflips.

Pride that even they couldn't resist our nation's allure.
Singing and dancing to Kompa and Zouk.
Wondering why their own music
did not ignite movements
from the soul into the hips.
Watching our sweetness
makes them drool
with envy.

*There is fundamental love for Haiti*
*that flows in the very core of us.*
*But within that love,*
*rests an equal measure of woe.*

\*\*\*

I have a dream that one day
we will not whisper our own mother's name.
That we will no longer carry it with pain or shame.
That every time the world hears Haiti
it will be filled with fear and respect.

I have a dream that one day we will march with pride.
That we will break shackles like we did *an milwuisankat*.
That our children will grow educated,
and our mentality will no longer be poor.
That we will no longer seek refuge elsewhere,
because our land will provide welfare.
That we will once again be the force leading others,
not the stone that other countries throw around.

Fritzinie Lavoile

But that is all it will be...just a dream.
If we do not cease tearing each other down.
Put our focus towards ending the oppression.
Stopping the demolition, stopping the rape,
No more violence, no more spreading of hate.
One member's progress
is one step closer to an end to our nation's distress.
Let us not forget what is written on our flag.

Let us enforce!
*"L'union Fait La Force".*

\*\*\*

# In the Wake
of Calamity

My back pressed against the cold metal chair. A gentle breeze passing through the open door, caressing my child-like figure. My tiny hands maneuvering the pen across the paper… tracing the bold black letters of my Tuesday homework. Anxiously waiting for my afternoon meal to be served.

In the kitchen, the fragrant blend of *epis, lay, avec zonyon* permeated the air. Sizzling and swirling in the mix of hot oil. A recipe known to every Haitian. Wondering how a smell could carry so many memories, so many overwhelming feelings of joy. Reminiscing on how good the *diri a legume* was going to taste. Anticipating the flavors that would dance upon my tongue. Breathing life into my taste buds. It's as if I could physically feel the joy coursing throughout my body. But slowly my smile began to fade, as I realized the shaking wasn't my own.

The beautiful plates I excitedly had arranged on the table. Their fragments were now scattered upon the concrete floor. My brain registered what was happening before my eyes, and I understood what I needed to do. But for a moment, frozen by an indescribable fear, I watched as the serenity of my Tuesday afternoon transformed into the most terrifying experience of my six years of life.

*"Poukisa nap tanmblé?"* I questioned, hoping for an answer different from my thoughts. *" Yon tranbleman tè Fritzou,"* came the reply, tinged with fear. Grabbing my hand, the rapid pounds of our feet hitting the earth running from an invisible force surrounding us. Not knowing which way to run. As if by some orchestrated fate, the unimaginable weight of a crumbling wall fell upon us.

Piercing shards of glass lacerated our skin. Blood trickling from my ears, tracing a path down my neck. Falling numb to the pain, seconds dragging like decades. Trying to push it off but to no use. Our feeble hands were of no match for the force that held us captive.

Amidst the chaos, everyone trampled upon us. Desperate to survive, oblivious to our cries. A man ran to us, I assumed he heard our desperate cries for help. Attempting to pull us out, even his strength faltered beneath the crushing weight. One became two and two became four pooling their strength; they managed to extract us from the wreckage. My shivers turned warm, taking comfort in their arms. Fear transitioned into love. The bruises on my body paled in comparison to their tender kisses.

\*\*\*

My world always appeared stagnant.
As if life were slipping away from me.
I, merely an observer
excluded from actively participating.
Just breathing and moving,
with the belief that my existence was mundane.

But that day, that moment
amidst the trembling of the earth:
the pillars that held our dreams
reservoirs of hope
came crashing down.

That moment after
the earth rattled my soul
left behind a profound silence
a profound stillness.

\*\*\*

I wander the earth's surface aching for freedom.
Longing to drift into the realm of my dreams.
Fleeing like startled rats, seeking a way.
Through mazes of life, we race, we chase.
In the quiet corners, we hide, we evade.

A secret wish to be like leaves on the wind.
Unburdened, untethered, not pinned.
We are all hiding within holes
that we find and create.
Digging. Digging. Digging.
Deep. Deep. Deep.

Our secrets are held by the earth.
A silent witness to our hidden pain.
The earth retains our fears.
It whispers stories.
It echoes all that we repress
in the rustling leaves and falling tears.

***

The taste of hope grew dim.
The essence of life felt distant and grim.
The future held no weight.
The present was only marked by passing days.

One foot in front of the other.
One breath after another.
Moving forward only to trick the mind
into thinking the body was still alive.

The soul was cognizant that it was not filled with life.

\*\*\*

Days melded into nights, and nights into days.
I'm not sure how long we slept under those tents.
Up to five hundred of us
a collective of survivors on a sodden field.
I imagined that our country
had transformed into a survivor camp
terrorized and living on rations.

The muddy ground beneath our feet
mirrored the turmoil within.
Supporting one another
through the trials that befell us,
discovering unity amidst the calamity.
Though the weight of tragedy
bore heavily upon our shoulders,
we refused to succumb to despair.
We looked beyond the muddy field,
onto the horizon.

\*\*\*

I blew the stars away
because I like how the sky looks
without them taking up space.

For sometimes, it is in the absence of illumination,
that we can truly appreciate the tranquility,
and revel in the quiet magnificence of serene vastness.

\*\*\*

There is something to be said about tragedy and the message that it leaves for those who survive its wake. There are those who choose to hit the reset button. As if the past were but a fleeting dream, to shield themselves from the haunting of its echoes. There are those who bear the weight of their experiences. Recognizing that acknowledging the past can be a catalyst for growth, compassion, and change. It is an act of courage to acknowledge the pain and loss while forging a path forward.

*Resilience takes many forms.*

\*\*\*

When I stepped off that plane
I not only stepped away from Haiti
but from friends and family.
I stepped away from memories.
Coming with my mind emptied.

Years would pass before I delved into the depths
of my formative years spent in Haiti.
To uncover the layers that had remained untouched.
To confront the lingering silence that followed the tragedy.

***

A desire for solitude prevails
walking alone, through silence, my way.
Neither fully alive nor courting death's doorsteps.

Tranquility, not the soothing peace's reign.
But the eerie quiet where thoughts remain.

No thrill in the senses, just routine in pace.
No motivation's spark, just a fog in my head.

Sleep remains distant, it's me and this bed.
My thoughts on my phone, where they're often led.
A cocoon of aloneness, where words linger unspoken.

***

Poetry becomes my prayer.
A melody for words that my vocal cords can't declare.
A way to unveil my devotion to the world.
I devote my mind to finding beauty in everything.
I devote my mind to paying attention to all that seems dull.

When my thoughts overflow, I tilt my head.
A river of words spills out of my ear.
Forming verses onto the pages.

Let them reach you.
Let me etch these words in your mind.
Let me empty my soul into yours.

***

My whole life I've felt submerged.
Drowning in the depths of unconsciousness.
Merely going through the motions...

Only now, I feel more awake.
More aware of my situation.
More in control of the water.

Yet, the shore remains elusive...

\*\*\*

I have left the taste of
different versions of myself
in everyone that I've met.

With every step taken, I shed a part of me.
Each fresh start an opportunity to adapt and evolve.
Crafting a new persona to fit the surroundings.

I wonder,
What could I build with all the pieces I've scattered?

\*\*\*

I feel like a shapeshifter.
I can't recall the number of times I've changed myself.
The many personalities that have cycled in.
Wearing a different version of myself with everyone.
Changing into what I thought they would like best.
Changing my smile. My hair. My clothes.
Morphing into my mini environments.

Are we all shapeshifters crawling in the skin?
Are we all sewn together by others?
Are we all molded into how they want us to be?

\*\*\*

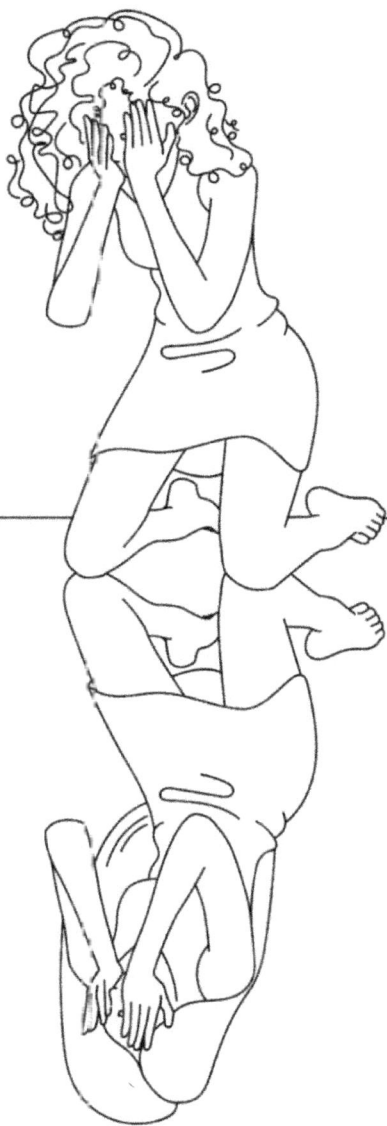

The crack in the ceiling opened, a piece of glass or paint dropped down. I looked up because of a sound I heard. One to two seconds was all it took for that piece from the ceiling to drop down and hit my eye like an arrow that had been waiting to be released.

I ran to the nearest sink, which was the kitchen sink. Filling my hands with water, trying to wash it out, it does nothing. Puckered my lips and tried to blow it out, it does nothing. I ran to the bathroom looking for a mirror, *I have to get a closer look*. I moved up to the mirror until my breath fogs it up. Using both my hands to spread my eye. Why is it the left one that always takes the direct hit?

As I'm looking for the piece of ceiling, maybe paint or drywall or brick wall, as I'm looking at the source of all my physical pain… I take my other fingers and try to take it out, it does nothing. I rummage through the drawers, trying to find tweezers, amid my blurry vision, I find it, still, it does nothing.

The only thing that the water, the air from my puckered lips, the mirror, my fingers, my hands, the tweezers, the only thing they did was create the river of tears that might as well have been blood.

\*\*\*

I want to stop the world from spinning so I can have a moment to breath. A moment to dive into my mind and pick out the parts that are hurting. Maybe reverse the spin of the world so I can go back and redirect my pasts. But, that's not a job for a human like me. I can only pray that my mask lasts a little longer so I can tidy up behind the scenes and make it look more presentable.

\*\*\*

Swallowed my true self.
Pushed it down my stomach.
Hoping if I pressed it down
long enough it would condense into nothing.
I let the world define me, dictate who I should be.
No, worse, I let it convince me
that I didn't know who I was.

\*\*\*

It saddens me that it's taken me this long to shed off the
weight condensing my inner being. That part of me, the
guiding light, that reassured me of my worthiness. That
whispered: *"You are enough, you are not meant to conform to their
expectations."*

\*\*\*

Our greatest weapon against stress is our ability to choose one thought over another. Catch yourself when you're having negative thoughts and turn them around.

\*\*\*

When true love blooms
we recognize the scars
yet our love doesn't diminish.

Let us extend this tenderness to ourselves.
Treating our souls as cherished soul mates.
Learning the art of self-love.
Learning how to love ourselves anyway.

***

In moments of reverie, I ponder a world without me.
Would I have even left a mark?
How swiftly would I be replaced, my absence erased?

We seek to be unique and special.
But if everyone's standing tall, can one be seen at all?
In this sea of souls, am I but a drop in human tide?

Let's not forget, in God's grand design
each life has a purpose, a story to share.
That is the symphony of our lives.
Where every note, every voice, contributes to the end.

So even if doubts and questions cloud the view,
know that you matter, your presence is valued.
You're like a thread in fabric,
pull one, and the whole tapestry goes undone.

\*\*\*

I often found myself wondering why I survived while two hundred and fifty thousand did not. Why did those men go out of their way to save us when there were many in the same position, stuck, yelling out for help, but remained unheard? Same school, same age, but not the same outcome. Same blood, same country, yet its very fabric torn. Homes collapsed, hearts shattered, yet God chose to preserve mine.

Over time I learned to stop questioning, as I figured out the best possible answer. He chooses our paths, and we must make the best of them. I will forever remember the bedrock from which I emerged, I will always cherish the memories of my best friend and the multitude of lives lost that day. I will carry them with me throughout my journey. Not as a burden but as a catalyst to strive for betterment and success. To fulfill the purpose for which I was saved.

\*\*\*

Dear God,

I'm asking you to take this feeling of deep loneliness away. This feeling of doubting the plan you have for me. This feeling of not deserving of this life. This feeling of dread on my heart. Of self-doubt, of depression, of unresolved trauma.

Replace it with a sense of belonging. I'm asking you to guide me towards emotional connections with the people around me. Towards a stronger relationship with you. Replace it with strong faith in your love for me.
Let your presence fill my heart in all that I pursue. Let your presence overflow within me, drowning out all the spirits of self-destruction. Let your grace flow out of me into all that surrounds me.

In your name I pray,
Amen

\*\*\*

# Mirrored Whispers

Dear daughter,

Everything I have asked the lord to give you, he gave you poetically. I asked him to cleanse you of all the bad parts of me, he gifted you the best parts of me. I asked him to keep you safe, to keep you in a glass house where not even a speck of dust can get to you. where you would be shielded from my own flaws and missteps. He placed an ocean between us. you found yourself on distant shores. I remained worlds apart.

Love,
mom

\*\*\*

Fritzinie Lavoile

In my dreamscape, you'd always be near.
Turning my nightmares into beautiful visions.
Always with the most stunning depictions.

A beautiful field of grass,
where prophets speak of a soon to come blessing.

In dark alleys where horrid creatures appeared.
Here you come, my brave butterfly fluttering with grace.
Fighting off horrors, chasing away every hint of fear.

\*\*\*

Dear mom,

No love could ever replace that of a mother. The unspoken agreement that you are protected, defended, understood.

Real love, that was nurtured in the womb along with every part of you. Comfort is never a question. Choosing you first, without a second thought.

No matter how much others may care, it will never translate the same. When you don't feel love from your parents whether it's because they're too far away emotionally or physically or both...

That is a void that the entire world cannot fill.

Love,
Fritzinie

***

I do not know
what it feels like to be dolled up by a mother.
She never taught me to apply makeup or style my hair.
There were no lessons on how to shave my legs.

*I had to learn to stop the bleeding all by myself.*

\*\*\*

How can you touch me and still be able to lift your hands?
Why doesn't yours feel as heavy, as reluctant as mine?

\*\*\*

My mom believes that I emerged into this world with fortune already wrapped around my foot. Her pregnancy, a solitary road, uncertain, she pondered ways to take back control. Thoughts turned into attempts turned into actions. Three times she wrestled with fate.

"Te gen moman," she said, "lè tout bagay te sanble pèdi, Mwen pat konn kijan anyen te pral mache. Kijan mwn te suppose mennenw nan mond sa.

Mwen pat posede anyen. Mwen pat ni gen rad ni gen manje pou ou. Mwen pat pare pou m vin yon manman."

She said:
"Malgre tout bagay say yo, lesprim te toujou rete bien kalm. Lèm fin akouche nan lopital la mwen we pou ki rezon. Tout sa ou te ka bezwen te gentan la ap tann ou."

***

I traced the placements of the moles of her face.
How can imperfections be placed so tenderly?
Her skin, a sanctuary where shadows seek refuge.
A deep dark that runs smoothly.
Her thighs gave strength to her stride
revealing purpose to every step.
Her resting face seemed unkind
only because she was reflecting
what the world expressed to her.
When she smiled her teeth secretly misaligned.
But still, her smile held beauty's charm.
Her voice, high pitched yet elegantly soft.

*She is as much of me as I am of her.*

\*\*\*

No one can ever erase
the love that a daughter has for her mom.
Even through her absence
If she pierced me with her knifes edge,
I would see beyond the blood.
To her attempts to mend my wounds.

***

Such a foreign feeling... I must confess,
To witness a mother and father inseparable
A world unknown to me... I must confess.
Longing to set foot in the realm
where their love does coalesce.

*　*　*

I have never come to know a complete household.
It's as if my sight is cursed, unable to envision.
My ears deprived of echoes of sweet words.
My tongue burnt, tasting only bitterness in this space.
Hands untouched... the presence of love I long to feel.
An undeserving heart, burdened by ordeal.
My mind, the only place where dreams reveal,
the warmth and reprieve a family should hold dear.

\*\*\*

What happens when the only thread
two people share is their child?
Regret simmers in the pot
they use to brew resentment.
Friction ignites a series of insults.
That tension taints the word family.

That child becomes a buffer, caught in the crossfire.
Her innocence fractured, she is split into two shields.
Concealing the wounds, they got from each other.

She becomes the well
where they pour each other's secrets.
The fountain they use to store their emotions.
The luck they both share.

\*\*\*

The perks of being my father's daughter:
You're his best friend, everywhere he goes you go.
As a baby his stomach was your safe place.
You've been handing him the tools while tears down and
rebuild his cars for as long as you can remember,
He cooks your favorite meals.
He styles your hair for school.
Carries you uphill, to avoid mud on your shoes.
He goes hungry so you could eat.
Every night he stays up with you doing homework.
Your love language is sharing music.
He is your biggest bully and cheerleader.
He still dances with the world crumbling on top of him.
You watched him renovate your first home,
Rushing to the ER as he almost blew off his finger.
Quality time is spending all night watching movies.
He drives you to your college dorm.
You went furniture shopping for your second home.
You bought your first car together.
He tells you all about his relationship drama.
He always celebrates your birthdays,
even when it's just the two of you.
He's turned everything you thought impossible, possible.

\*\*\*

My father tells me that he was raised with no love.
He said:
*"Lew nan misè ou pa gen tan pou lanmou."*

He raised me with the kind of love
that could not be taught or replicated.
The kind of love that doesn't need to be forced.
The kind of love that doesn't grow tired.
The kind of love that makes you feel safe.
The kind of love that every
parent should have for their children.

My father tells me that he wasn't raised on love.
But he raised me to love
everyone around me.

My father broke the cycle of savagery.
I too will raise my children with love.
I too will teach them how to love.

\*\*\*

I wish I could be like a wall.
Cast stones at me
Left with no a dent.
But I'm not. I'm sensitive.
like a sponge. I absorb
every thought
every emotion.
They ruminate on my mind.
I push them down until
they become too much for my tiny figure...
until I am forced to release.
Then, I explode
into tears,
into poetry,
into art.

\*\*\*

Do your future children a favor. Don't bring them into a world with you unstable. A child should not be the one to help you reach stability and growth. A child should not be the one to pave the way. Or endure your anger like night endures day.

A child isn't meant to bear your angry blows or join you on a healing journey. You should be whole and healed.

*Let them grow in a world of love and care.*
*Where anger and pain are not theirs to bear.*
*Create a nurturing environment.*
*Where their potential blooms*
*like flowers in the air.*

\*\*\*

Be vulnerable to your children.
Show them that you too are human.

Be vulnerable to your children.
Let them swim in the depths of your heart.

Be vulnerable to your children.
Let them know you too
have emotions that ebb and flow.

Let them see your emotions in their different ways.
To know it's okay to have feelings that come and sway.

Be vulnerable for your children.
So, they can see there is strength in being open.
So, they don't mistake your passion for anger.
And weakness in their vulnerability

\*\*\*

I see the pain in his eyes,
yet he smiles when he sees me.
He is the bravest man I know.
Countless nights working hard.
Seeing the disappointment in his eyes.
Hearing the mistreatment he gets at work.
Slowly but surely checking off
one dream after the other.

Whenever I feel like giving up,
I look back at the progress my dad has made
and the sense of defeat blows over me.

\*\*\*

*I wonder if they know they have art in common.*
As they ask themselves whatever drew them to each other.
Thinking of all that they loathe about one another.

*I wonder if they know they have art.*
Lingering underneath their fingernails.
As my mother tells me of her passion for theater
and I am learning the lines to perform her play.

*I wonder if they know.*
How rare a treasure it is to come in harmony creating life.
As my father's hands grip the steering wheel
reminiscing of his lost love for poetry.
and I am telling him how I wish to never lose mine.

*I wonder.*
If it was ever meant to be any other way.
As they speak to me as if the other didn't exist.

*I.*
A living mural of their artistry.
A grand tapestry of fates display
of how two worlds can collide
and as quickly drift away.

\*\*\*

79

# Subtle Blessings

I recall the days when my grandma would come visit me in Haiti. We would sit beneath the hot sun where the gentle breezes blew. I would mold her silver hair with wrists that would twist, and fingers that'd weave cornrows like fine art.

Her head, a canvas painted with tales. Each braid was more precious than it seemed. In every parted line I laid tracks to the past. With every strand carefully woven and placed my imagination explored her scalp.

Braiding wasn't just patterns. It held a language so strong it carried through generations.

Even today, as I shape my own strands, I bear our traditions.

*Each twist, every coil*
*is a statement I wear.*
*A tribute to our history,*
*a story I declare.*

\*\*\*

My grandmother carries me in her back pocket arming herself with my language. On the bus, in the store, in a taxi, navigating the roads of this country. All because I could translate...

\*\*\*

I am the first-born child.
The only child.
The immigrant child.
The child of immigrants.
I cannot afford to have mediocre dreams.

\*\*\*

People have hidden in planes.
Drowned in oceans.
Given up all they've known.
Waited for decades.
Spilled sweat, blood, tears.
All to reach where I stand
I cannot take any of it for granted.

\*\*\*

Both of my parents are big dreamers. They instilled in me the same. They encouraged me to strive. To get the best grades. To be the best. To not be happy with mediocrity.

*That is not enough for them.*
*That is not enough for me.*

\*\*\*

A child of an immigrant's biggest fear lies in feeling unworthy of the sacrifice that was made in the name of their future. To see their parents' efforts all in vain. Their pride tarnished, consumed by shame.

\*\*\*

Depression woke me up, its voice so cruelly sneered:

*"No one wants to hear what you have to say.*
*You're a burden, taking up too much space.*
*Alone and unloved, that's your only place.*
*You do not deserve to be happy.*
*You do not deserve to be understood."*

Closing my eyes, I drift back to sleep.
Hoping its bitterness will one day remold into sweetness.
Yearning for my mind to learn to treat me with kindness.

\*\*\*

Who knows you better than you do? Who tells you what you cannot pursue? Who teaches you self-doubt?

There is an I in enemies. It's there to remind us not all dangers are easily perceived. That subtlety can deceive. It's there to remind us to look in the mirror before pointing fingers. To not hesitate to challenge the intrusive thoughts. To understand that they don't have our best interest at heart.

For all the times that you are mad at your past self. Maybe dismayed for your past self for not realizing these earlier. Know those decisions were made because of the knowledge you lacked. There is no way for you to go
back and speak to your younger self. You can only store these words for your future self. Make peace with your younger self so your future self won't have to.

*Allow yourself to make mistakes.*
*That's the only way to grow.*

\*\*\*

As humans, we're imperfect through and through. Most of the time we make mistakes. Embrace the imperfections in others and yourself.

Don't let your past dictate your future path. You have the freedom to change, to grow, to craft yourself into the person you want to be. Use your origin to fuel your destination. Use your past to uplift, never to be held down.

\*\*\*

I've learned to forgive the past versions of myself and others. Witnessed many character changes in you and me, to understand that we are ever growing creatures.

*Let forgiveness flow like a healing psalm*
*from ourselves onto others.*

\*\*\*

Forgiveness is not tolerance. I may forgive but I won't tolerate any actions that cause me pain. Preserving my peace is always my aim.

\*\*\*

Even when I don't feel
loved by my family,
loved by the people around me,
love for myself,
I know that God loves me.
It overwhelms me.

\*\*\*

Father God,

You are my shield, my rock, and my fortress.
You are my lamp that keeps burning, guiding my way.
You are my strength and courage to face each day.

Arm me with endurance so that I may be able to handle
both the challenges that I create for myself and the ones that
the world throws my way.

Keep me focused on the things that matter, the battles that'll
help me grow. I don't want to entertain the thoughts that
leave my soul feeling drained.

Grant me just a piece of your love and grace so that I can
live like you, unafraid.

Love,
Fritzinie

\*\*\*

When the wind whispers
it softly reassures me,
*"You are alive. You are here."*
Echoing my rhythm, inspiring each breath.
Its caress on my cheeks
makes me feel something outside of myself.

In nature's language, it speaks to my soul.
Connecting me to a world where God is in control.
A reminder that I'm part of something grand.
With every gust it propels me forward.
With the wind as my companion, I will withstand.

\*\*\*

I treasure the truth of being molded from dirt.
Like the trees and grass, we sprouted from God's heart.
*When rooted in God, though the world may sway us,*
*It may even bend us but will never break us.*

\*\*\*

When crafting a song, you gather random notes.
Each one alone, not striking, not quite appealing.
Yet, when entwined they form a symphony.
Creating harmony, like lovers holding hands.

No matter how they are shuffled,
placed in different orders,
every chord finds its place to make sense.

Just like your life
no matter how you are rearranged,
you will adapt and learn to flow.
When you can't find which line you belong to
know that you are a perfect fit wherever you stand.
At each stage of your life you move,
drop down a line or rise up a line your song evolves.
The notes find a way to fit together.

*＊*

Who is the world to tell me how big I can grow?
I will break the atmosphere if I have to.

\*\*\*

Future immigrants
when you come here
keep your head high.
Remember your purpose.
Your goal is greatness.
Nothing is out of your reach.

You are not less valuable.
You are not less intelligent.
You are brave.
You are bold.
You are here to make a difference.
For yourself, your family, the world.

***

The essence of life is to make your younger self smile. Not to compete or compare your journey with others. Remember when innocence thrived, and magic was real.

Keep that youthful lens, dare to dance without constraint. No need to compare, no need to outdo. Just follow your path, improving a little each day. Trust me when I say, your inner child is already in awe of you.

***

When we take a moment to look around us the good may be hard to see. Most blessings are not apparent. Not clear of what it is we're supposed to be grateful for.

When we take a moment to look around us let's make sure to pick up on our subtle blessings.

Our relationships with the people around us. A smile from a stranger. The simple things that make our day.

They seem so insignificant. We don't recognize they form the blueprints of many prayers.

***

For all the tears
there were repairs.
All the bumps on the road
helped to propel us forward.

Let the whispers of sweet gratitude
flow off your lips everyday
along with the rhythm of your heartbeat.
Thanking God for the privilege of a life
for every second is a miracle.

\*\*\*

# Glimpses of Home

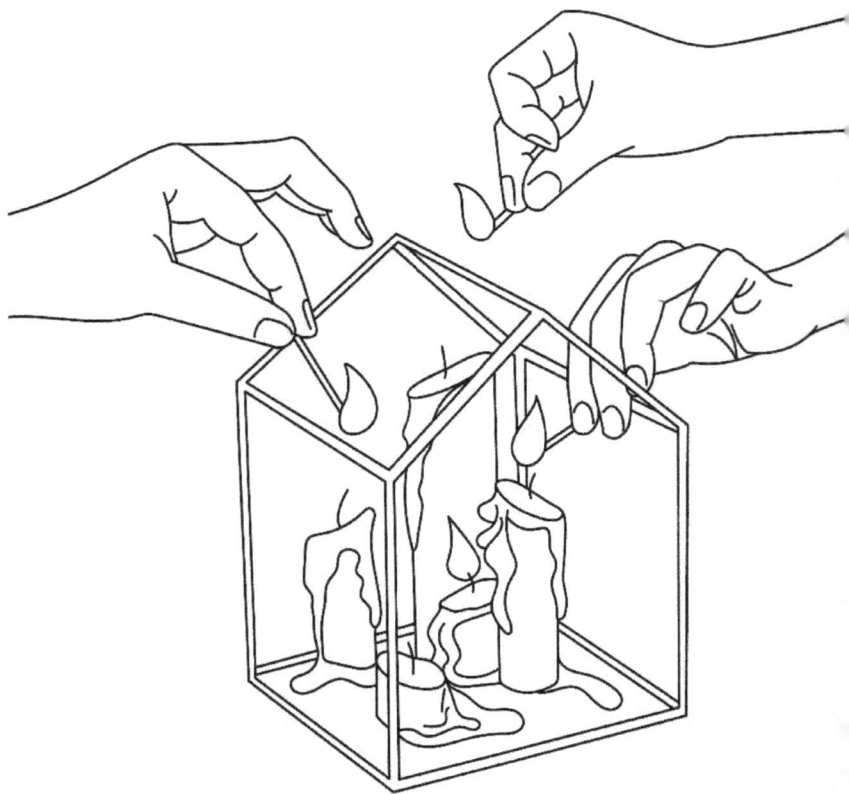

Fritzinie Lavoile

Tell me that my voice will start a choir chanting so loud
that it will bring silence to whispers of fear and doubt.

That my tears will melt into streams of rivers, into tides of
oceans, into waves of hurricanes that break through
chains.

That my soft whistle will blow into tornado winds whose
spins control destructive forces that lay our land.

That my pen will never run out of ink, and my fingers will
never cramp. That my creations won't die from old age.

That I will dig tunnels so deep into souls that it goes
through their future and reaches into their past.

When my bare and buried body is leeching into the ground
I will breed titans of flowers.

At the heart of the forest my gardens will grow
past millions of lifetimes.

I will be blowing kisses to God
for the gift of my eternal life.

\*\*\*

How remarkable we are!
To be able to twist our tongues and mold our words.
To have different versions of ourselves spill out
depending on who we are talking to.
Masking our true voice with them
but speaking freely among our own.
It sounds to me like they're the outsiders
struggling to grasp the unity within these borders.

No matter how they mimic our speech,
It never sounds quite right as it flows off their tongues.
Their imitation's easy to detect.
As if they wish to colonize our shared space,
claim our expressions, make them theirs.
Yet failing to capture the essence or finesse.

How can it be we speak English more refined
Then those born within these borders?
Why label me uneducated, a black girl from Haiti.
When I wield your language with grace.
Bending it to convey my every will.

***

There is a place that holds magic
day and night.
The spirit of this nation,
rich and bright.
Full of wonder and delight.

The music, sweet and bold.
It enters your ears
makes its way into your toes.

Painted with the darkest hues.
From the brown of the soil to the black of its people.
To the red of the blood, royal ancestry flows.

From the rolling hills to the forest lands.
There's a place for everyone to take a stand.
From the talking of the drums,
to the singing of praise.
Here lies vibrant culture.
Here lies pride.
Here lies a land of gold.

\*\*\*

Hidden in our complexion is a treasure to behold.
Secrets that will take you out of this dimension.

Black as the soil that sustains.
We are gentle as droplets of rain.
Our Skin continues to glow
even when the sun has reached its highest point.

Moisturized and shiny,
our melanin tells a story
of travels up hills through rough terrains
of triumphs against the wind.

Carved with elegant strokes of stretch marks,
each line represents the road to salvation,
from the frustration of this nation.

This back says it all.
It stands tall throughout all the odds.

You say black is beautiful.
I say to define black in one word is - unfathomable.
That's like every spec of sand - immeasurable.

Even the sun applauds black beauty with warm smiles
leaving proof of its love in different tones.

***

Everywhere we witness gilded kings and queens forging
paths, breaking generational curses.

Let us stave off black trauma.
No more succumbing to the white man's narrative.

We will raise our flags of victory.
Listen to the cheering of our people-
This is not the time for self-doubt or degradation.

We are warriors.
We are exemplars of greatness.
We are black and we are proud.
No more will we whisper.
No more will we bow.
We are black and we are proud.

*We celebrate our excellence long past any allotted time.*

\*\*\*

Whenever I encounter an immigrant family,
whenever my Uber driver's English is not fluent,
my heart leaps with pride.

I want to tell them how deeply they're admired.
I want to tell them how much I cannot wait
for their dreams to transpire.

But, how do I communicate
that there's no need to prove their worth to me?
For I sensed their value overflowing
the instant out gaze met.
How can I make them understand
my unwavering belief in their abilities?

*While the world might view them as lesser,*
*I see reflections of myself, my father.*
*I see traces of bravery, courage, and boundless potential.*
*I see greatness that cannot be encapsulated*
*by any men-built walls.*

\*\*\*

We, the children of immigrants,
Must carve out a seat at the table, even if it's denied.

We, the children that are immigrants,
Must persevere without apology for our existence.

We must persist despite the odds.
In a world that often overlooks our stories.

We must be our own advocates.

*For us, who lack established paths to follow,*
*With no guiding hands to navigate this maze,*
*must, in turn  become the guide for others.*

\*\*\*

When you arrive here, do not fear starting anew. Don't hesitate to work in factories or take on roles such as janitors or drivers. Should someone belittle you, calling you "stupid" for imperfect English, do not be offended. For your genius shines in your own language.

Reclaim your power through hard work and pride. Never let them see you ashamed of your roots. Brave the challenges of being the pioneer. Embrace the art of mastering patience, for these trials are but temporary steppingstones on your remarkable journey.

\*\*\*

I remember the days spent in one-bedroom apartments. My dad and I crafted chicken noodle soup because it was all we had.

The excitement welled up when my grandma would send them from America. At the time, I didn't even know their name. It marked the first fragment of my future that I truly adored. Slicing pieces of hotdog or chicken to jazz them up, turning them into thrilling concoctions. And they were indeed thrilling.

Whether in Haiti, Florida, or New York.

Whether dwelling in our sturdy concrete-built home, our modest one-bedroom apartment, or our very first house in America.

\*\*\*

We immigrant children often shoulder a unique burden. One that encompasses the wellbeing of our families back home and the land we left behind.

At every juncture, we're reminded that while we managed to cross the sea and brave the bridge, countless others weren't granted the same opportunity.

Even before our roots have firmly settled into foreign soil, before our aspirations find full scope, before we can bear the fruits of our endeavors, the echoes of responsibility reverberate. It underscores our duty to extend our hands to those we left behind, to provide help and support.

***

This is my reminder to you that it's okay to take care of yourself first. It's okay to say no.

For us, the first-generation immigrants, our foremost task is to construct our foundations here. Nurturing our mental well-being is paramount, prioritizing our own welfare before extending the lifeline and forging bridges for others to cross.

The finest aid stems from securing our own life vests. Crafting an environment in which others can truly thrive, so they don't face ground zero, as you once did.

This isn't selfish; it is strategy. For how can they navigate the journey across treacherous waters if no one stands ready to anchor the distant shore?

\*\*\*

A decade has passed in this country.
I spent nine years in Haiti.
Does this mean that I am more American than Haitian?
More of here than I am of there?

After all these years,
This land still carries a hint of unfamiliarity.
Haiti still feels like home.

\*\*\*

There are those who choose to stay.
Whether it's out of fear for a new beginning
or faith that their country will get better.

There are those who choose to stay.
Not looking for better elsewhere.
Those that are comfortable in their country
no matter the state.

\*\*\*

Our minds hold remarkable power over us. If left unguarded it often steers us down uncharted paths. I chuckle at the narratives my mind conjures; those routes it could lead me on when untamed.

For the longest stretch, I deluded myself into believing I could never truly own anything. During those days, most of my attire and shoes were all hand-me-downs and the idea of truly possessing something seemed distant.

I wasn't residing in a house of my own, nor a room, nor a bed. The fridge and the couch didn't belong to me. Amidst this, my dad's advice echoed in my ears: *"pa janm fè jalousi pou sa lot moun posedé. Tan lè a rive wap jwen sak pou ou an"* Yet, to my 12-year-old mind that seemed impossibly far away.

\*\*\*

Dear God,

Let it be your plan unfolding, clear for me to see. Even when
I cannot clearly see Lord help me to take the actions that are
indeed part of your plan. For your timing is divine,
everything will find its place.

Guide my steps, Lord, through every phase.
Illuminate my path with your loving gaze.
May I embrace each moment, big and small.
As Your perfect design encompasses all.

Grant me patience, as I navigate each bend.
A faithful heart, on your guidance Lord I depend.
With trust in your will I humbly pray,
Lead me forward Lord in each and every way.

Love,
Fritzinie

\*\*\*

I believe one of the most profound lessons my dad taught me was that hand-me-downs have an expiration date. He ingrained in me the understanding that undertaking tasks we'd rather avoid, including the less glamorous jobs, enduring disrespect, and weathering mistreatment, all contribute to the realization of our dreams. He showed me that our aspirations are in a state of becoming, and we must persist through the process.

He emphasized that our primary audience should be ourselves, not others. Our dreams, the seeds we sow, are ours alone to nurture and transform into tangible realities.

***

To all the beds that I have slept in yet were not mine. All the rooms that cradled me but were not called mine.

To all the pieces of furniture I might have rearranged but were not mine.

To all the ceilings that watched me rest sheltering my dreams through the years:

I have finally found my way home.

\*\*\*

As we walk along the pavement and feel the breeze blow, we encounter each other through the foundation. Rocky or smooth, dirt roads or concrete. Promenading to the park, office, school, or factory.

That foundation connects bridges from across the sea. That foundation grows trees from around the world. There's no telling how many stories are rustling through the leaves. In that harmony we create movements, working to compose a never-ending peace.

We have all come to know the bitterness of sorrow. Where we were asking ourselves- when will it be over? When will this darkness fade lighter? We are all at a juncture where everything is changing, from our climate down to our being. But we endure it like no other. With the hope that our tears did not stream in vain. That our children's hearts will become strangers with pain.

We covered it with love. Shared our compassion through a simple gaze in each other's eyes. Communicating that we have all lost something. Whether it was opportunity or the touch of a loved one's once warm hand- now covered in layers of dirt and coldness.

We catch the desperate search for progression. Striving for a solution to stop the deterioration of our nation. It is that love that holds open the door to a smile. That cool breeze that carries the whispers of- merci, thank you, shalom, gracias, namaste, traveling to sooth our minds. Always on one foundation, earth.

***

As we walk onto different paths,
we embrace each other's pasts.

Endeavoring to improve
the conditions that we inherited.

It is that determination
that tells us to do better for each other.

To keep on leading, building,
discovering, learning, and teaching.

To begin every morning with the sharp belief
that everything will be made better,
as long as we keep stepping together.

\*\*\*

Look at how life has treated you,
look at the art you were able to create despite it.

# ACKNOWLEDGEMENT

As I stand at the completion of this poetry collection, I am profoundly grateful to God for illuminating my path and infusing my words with purpose. This journey has been a testament to the power of life experiences as the wellspring from which my creativity flows.

Thank you to my parents, whose unwavering belief in me has allowed me to pursue my passion. I am immensely grateful to my friends, whose endless conversations, critiques, and encouragement have helped shape my thoughts and refine my ideas.

Thank you to Angel Nduka-Nwosu, my dedicated editor. Janni Pillerva, my brilliant illustrator who lent visual life to these words.

Lastly, to you, my readers-both known and unknown-I extend my heartfelt thanks.

In every word I penned
and every line you read,
a piece of my heart resides.

-Fritzinie

.

www.ingramcontent.com/pod-product-compliance
Lightning Source LLC
Chambersburg PA
CBHW021011090426
42738CB00007B/745